SHATTER THE GLASS, SHARDS OF FLAME

SEPT 2018

DEAR TOM,

PLEASE GIVE MY BEST WISHES TO MY CHARLBURY FRIENDS. I MISS YOU ALL TERRIBLY.

YOUR CANADIAN BROTHER,

ART

SOME OF THESE POEMS HAVE PREVIOUSLY APPEARED IN PRINT

Crows; Mise en abyme; A Prayer for Cold Hands; Heard at
Dave Mullally's Wake: Souris River PEI; Guilt; Ivy the Belly
Dancer, *The Nashwaak Review*, 2017.
To the girl who stole my guitar; Oneida Schoolboys;
Last Name, *Prairie Fire*, 2017.
Salamatu, *Queen's Quarterly,* 2017.
Playing Chess with Mohammad; The New Neighbours,
Queen's Quarterly, 2016.
Stevedores, *The Dalhousie Review*, 2016.
Sea King, *QWERTY*, 2015.
I didn't come here to write poems; Rugby; Tragedy, Ruah,
and Whiskey; Skye; Jim Smith, *The Nashwaak Review*, 2015.
Hurricane, *Queen's Quartely*, 2015.
May I Use You As a Reference; My First Protest a Snow
Angel; The Bomb Makers; Lip Twitch; Love Letter
to a Soldier, *Boston Poetry Magazine*, 2015.
Warrant Officer Hawko, *Vallum*, 2014.
Memento Mori, *The Dalhousie Review*, 2013.
Unmarked Grave, *The Antigonish Review*, 2011.

Shatter the Glass, Shards of Flame

Poems

Gerald Arthur Moore

| N₁ | O₂ | N₁

CANADA

*Publisher's note: This book is a work of fiction. Names, characters, places and
incidents are either the product of the author's imagination or are used
fictitiously, and any resemblance to actual persons living or dead
is entirely coincidental.*

LIBRARY AND ARCHIVES CANADA CATALOGUING IN PUBLICATION

Moore, Gerald Arthur, 1972–, author
Shatter the glass, shards of flame / Gerald Arthur Moore.

Poems.
ISBN 978–1–988098–66–1 (softcover)

I. Title.

PS8626.O5937S53 2018   C811'.6   C2018–904209–5

Printed and bound in Canada on 100% recycled paper.

NOW OR NEVER PUBLISHING
901, 163 Street
Surrey, British Columbia
Canada V4A 9T8

NONPUBLISHING.COM
Fighting Words.

We gratefully acknowledge the support of the Canada Council for the Arts
and the British Columbia Arts Council for our publishing program.

Dedicated to Mark Sampson

Poet, novelist, and soul brother

To the Girl Who Stole My Guitar

My paranoid neighbour's video recording .
is grainy, but I can see your short white coat, blonde hair,
shoulder-checking-nervousness. You are holding my sunburst
Larrivee guitar.

Even from this distance, across the furry grey street,
the pixilated lawn that is mostly dandelion, you are standing
there,
keeping lookout for your boyfriend or pimp,
as he loads my pillow cases with bottles of scotch.

My neighbour's lawn is perfect—he strangles
each new weed or plucks them by the root, and tosses them
on the blacktop to expire like a fish out of water.
He's disgusted by my indifference to dandelions
and my carelessness that leaves doors unlocked, or the guitar by
the window.
I see the yellow fiery bursts against the lawn as truth.
When they seed, I admire the floating paratroopers
that so bravely commit themselves to the wind.
The neighbour doesn't see the beauty in you either,
he only sees thief, prostitute, junkie.
He laughs that you appear to have
a black half-moon smiling and swelling
on your cheek, from where you've been punched.

I can see a lot in these fifteen seconds of distant footage,
before you meet your accomplice and walk down my driveway.
You don't play guitar, for example, the way you awkwardly
hold it.
My neighbour doesn't see, yours is a history of bruises;
nor does he see that you are a soft spoken poem,
a floating parasol in search of a whisper landing to fertile soil.

WARRANT OFFICER HAWKO
For Jason MacPhail

Crow-nosed,
cigar stub of a face, slaps blueberry pie
into an outstretched tin canteen cup like an insult.
Acting as if I was a freckle wristed Dickensian character
holding out a bowl for more.

Slams in sludge-brown army stew,
tills the muck with ladle;
churns it until the mess-kit metamorphosis
to the muds of Passchendaele.
"You like that? It's not for enjoyin' Moore,
It's fuel for killin'."

THE NEW NEIGHBOURS

The new neighbours arrived in the night
a frantic mandolin break of commotion;
one Malibu Classic taxi carried their lives
in the back bench seat,
and the trunk held a corrugated cardboard crib
with a rickety rasping asthmatic dog,
that dragged a back leg to my lawn
making the first of many minefield deposits.

A doomed boy dragged a solitary garbage bag
over the milk crate steps, and carried a bare bulb lamp—
the cord wrapped round his throat like a garrote.

The second time I saw him, he was a gargoyle
perched atop a snowbank on a school-day.
Said he'd missed the bus, and without boots
couldn't make it through all the slush
that comes between a boy and opportunity.

His mother was always in bed.

That perfect December day I rapped on his door,
and waited; he floated from darkness,
agreed to help me fashion a snowman.
It was his first. We marveled at the imprisoned chlorophyll
in the few strands of deep green summer grass,
exposed as we rolled the enormous thorax;
then built a ramp to get it atop the base orb:
Before we dug the ramp away,
I told him of the Roman's sloping road to Masada,
and the fortress at the flat top of the mountain;
how the rebel Israelites chose suicide over slavery.

The morning after we made the snowman
I woke to find my front yard occupied
like the ranks of a terracotta army,
whom were all facing the house;
frozen figures of funerary art
silent in their ranks,
Labbatt Blue bottlecap eyes, staring.

The boy must have worked under the full moon
scavenging pine cones accoutrements,
pikemen armed with broken hockey sticks,
old bricks as boots, red sashes
slashed from drapes, car mat armour,
each with a horsehair Salvador Dali moustache.

In spring, I hadn't realized they'd moved again,
until the flashing lights and sterile suits,
the push and suction pull of air filters;
emerging from the skeletal shed,
a makeshift mausoleum of exhausted timber
and torn tarpaper,
carrying out the decomposing dog,
now flat in his cardboard crib,
stepping over the frozen remains
of a defeated army on their battlefield.

MEMENTO MORI

He shouldn't be driving.
Slowly rumbles through the lot,
indecisive,
aiming his pick-up truck
here and then there,
with three types of paint
on the rusty bumper.

Gets out and gently closes the door,
then violently stabs the roof with a toilet plunger—
marking it for when he
trundles out of Walmart
with adult diapers and orange marmalade.

His memory is fading.
Soon he'll forget the hours of catch in the backyard
or setting up the sprinkler on hot days.
He'll forget the toys he made us
with those calloused hands;
the all too dangerous toboggan run
down the Niagara Escarpment.

He'll forget the poem he memorized
to impress me:
Childhood will drift up like an escaped kite.
His wife will evaporate like spilled gasoline.
I'll become city lights in the distance:
at first bright—an orange sky, then a pinprick
until, one day soon, I vanish
into the confusion of headlights and turnpikes,
pretty nurses and strange rooms.

JIM SMITH

Rolled his sleeves over his
Canadian Airborne tattoo, one arm pumping a ratchet:
Those wrinkled hands were awkward with cutlery
or teacup, more sure on beer bottles,
steady on stone saws.

I remember that he died in late April.
There were seventy-seven tulips at his funeral.
His hands were crossed like the Mona Lisa,
and his open casket smile was strange.

I'd been called upon to help fix a car.
The loose gravel in Jim's throat tumbled
when he cawed for me to
"Start 'er up."

I felt like a prince in canvas sneakers,
pushing Chuck Taylor footprints against the dashboard,
to see over the wheel of the Buick,
under the yawning hood—a proscenium arch.

"Turn 'er over."

I grabbed the key like a prize, rotated my hand:
There was a combining of gears as if a great muscle
were contracting;
the engine wound up, and roared.

Then he screamed,
"Turn it off! Turn it off!"
But I didn't know how.
There were several seconds of mad confusion;
the gravitas of the act–consequence nexus
revealed itself for the first time in my life.

Wrapping a hanky on it,
holding his hand as if it were a lemon square,
one digit dangling on a skin-hinge,
another was a deformed slug on the engine block.
He took that severed finger and
tossed it in the dog's bowl.

When he died that April, I picked tulips for his funeral,
his hands—one damaged, one not—were crossed
like the Mona Lisa,
and his smile seemed strange.

SKYE

Silent reading in class
Skye, a dark haired girl, in the third row, chooses to eat a carrot—
sounds like someone tapping icicles off an eaves trough,
the way it drops and pops
where almost everyone in the room
gives her a beleaguered glance
over the parapet of their novels,
save for the two future bikers
and one hipster, in his dark brown
vintage KGB leather.

She's a poet, and poets do as they do
it seems,
eat raw vegetables loudly so as to escape the noise
of quiet;
I join her clatter with a green apple,
waiting until her carrot has gone off
before starting my clomp and charge;
our duet never duels, it compliments,
one great crack followed by another,
and maybe, if the muses see fit,
some high school anthology will gather us
into its peach basket,
immortalizing our rhythmic distraction.

LIP TWITCH

It hung like the threat of crucifixion, on a nail
in the barn. I didn't know what it was for.

When the chain tightened over the mare's lip,
she reared and split, flowing,
bared teeth, grain spit, and blood.
They turned the stick over and
over, twisting that chain—too tight.
Red hanky bubble froth, falling.

Copious rivulets spilled, when she lifted her head;
thin dark ribbons, twisting
beautifully downward like fly tape,
her eyes were wide orbs
aiming hoofs that shot like pistons;
shaking off halter and hands.
If a horse can have resolve,
hers said, shoot me in the head
I'm never getting in that trailer again.

Appearing, from the crossed double doors,
standing in the transept of the barn,
like the ghost of Hamlet's father:
"What do you idiots think you're doing?"

Dad called for a shearing razor.
With work worn hands, he rubbed
the smooth steel, friction-warm;
clicked the switch so it hummed,
held the handle under her jaw line:
soothing; she let out a comfortable
whinny, the rage evaporated.

She flashed her black mane;
dropped a hatful of road apples.

Softly, "That's a girl. That's a girl."
Gently encouraged the harness, as if he was
leading her to the dance floor.

Hurricane

As the hurricane gets serious
the potted plant, a waxed leaf begonia
decides it can't take it anymore and jumps
off the end table, and breaks itself on the hardwood.

The air has changed and the choir of birds
no longer sing, they're panicked.
Every aged tree in the neighbourhood shakes,
preparing for the force, testing themselves;
but the old ones, the octogenarians, know.
They are going over to the other side tonight
and seem quietly resolved to their fate.

The seaside salt rain starts coming in heaving sheets,
and in the bluster and knuckles and destruction come,
like a drunk at Christmastime, when the paycheque
is gone, and the new lights flicker on the tree—purchased
by Mom without Dad's permission. All he sees
is the money we can't afford. So he becomes the storm,
and tears down the tree—and puts the heels of his work-boots
over the painted glass bulbs, and grinds them into
coloured grit on the floor.

As I sweep up the broken pot
the deep howl comes from within the storm,
the floorboards creak as the house leans
and we flinch.

The Banners at Drumcree

March this orange banner
          right through them;
                    the drums;
Remember the fallen.
          We have been bleeding for a hundred years.

Will they attack
          this sour parade?
                    It is our right.
Take back our history.
          We have been bleeding for a hundred years.

Set the time-fuses;
          they killed us last night;
                    innocent children, a woman.
Maintain our resolve,
          burn away your tears,
                    we have been bleeding for a hundred years.

The cobble
          was not laid
                    to give their boots rhythm.
Light the rags now and throw,
          shatter the glass, shards of flame,

before we kill,
          What is your name?

THE BOMB MAKERS

This morning there are scars on the road.
Dark circular petrol bomb bruises
ringed with blue and yellow, like punches.
Exploding pipes, jacks and rusty nails.
"Nobody died today from Belfast confetti"—
words disappear like incense into the din.
"It was just ladies purses at twenty paces."
But there are fragmentation marks on stones
and bones in Milltown Cemetery.

I Didn't Come Here to Write Poems

I didn't come here to write poems
about indifferent, soft-eyed horses
grazing the hills above mass graves
in Titanyen, far enough away,

the ditches look confetti strewn, like *papier mâché*;
throngs of flies whisper their final hymns,
rebar bones eviscerate cinderblock skin,
ruined staircases grin madly.

The stadium—a ribcage now:
A jawbone, torn from a face;
I kick dirt on it; protect it from the dogs,
cover it with a brick.

I'm an alchemist who turns Haiti's misery
into metaphor, but I swear,
standing atop piles of rubble that were homes,
that I didn't come here to write poems.

ANONYMOUS GRAVE

His swollen eyes dripping
With curds of infection,
That trickled down his dark cheeks
Like buttermilk;
Attracting flies, as if he were
A rotting corpse,
No longer a living man.

He drew his finger across his throat,
I've seen that sign too many times now;
It's not a threat in Haiti—
He was telling me that he is balancing,
Balancing on the edge of the razor,
Between another day
And the anonymous grave.

BAUDELAIRE

In the sea of blue tarps
this displacement camp
is a wasteland, hemorrhaging
outside Port-au-Prince.

With the flick-knife
my Haitian friend
uncaps stubbies;
pours out brown-glass solutions
like Creole poems.
Anyone who doesn't drink
he says, is an animal.

MARILYN RAYMER
for Yvonne Martin

In April, two months after the earthquake,
we found her medical bag
pressed beneath cruel rubble;
it appeared in the cinderblocks
like a black tongue.

Opened it, as if it were an ancient tomb,
unearthed the archaeological remains;
the spectacles, the medicine,
and a Bible with her name.

PAPILLION AND MR. BEAUTIFUL

Immediately awake and drowning
in the collapse of mosquito netting;
you called me Papillion as I emerged
from the sweat-tangled shrubbery of white silk,
head first, like butterfly tearing free of its cocoon.
You admired my metamorphosis.

We met her together, a little girl from Borel.
She had curiously red-smudged hair, like rust,
and shouted, "Blonde! Blonde!"
You said, "No, not Blonde. My name is Pierre."
She told me that you had laughing eyes,
"We call him Mr. Beautiful." I informed.
Her curious mob of friends took off our hats to examine us
more closely,
"And behold," you announced, "Here is Papillion." as if I were
a king.
She laughed with us, asked if we ate fried plantain and rice in
Canada,
notified us, in a dignified tone bursting with confidence, that
she was five.
Combed our heads, ran her small hands through our beards,
gently touched our cream skin and looked at fingers
to see if it would wipe off.

We left that village with deep and complicated slivers,
forever away, riding "tap-tap" trucks,
through palm groves, past the mass graves,
to the cinderblock mayhem of the earthquake zone.

Homes crushed and gutted, piles of immovable ruin,
Cite Soleil's street sluice, tent cities, acrid smoke,
garbage burning, oily ribbons of soot.
Port-au-Prince's coughing-black-snot desperation,
to a UN checkpoint, more plastic tarp displacement camps,
until we arrive, use the running password.
A guard with the short barrel shotgun opens the gate;
in a trance we drift behind the cinderblocks of our fortress.
Broken bottlenecks have been pressed into concrete at the top
like blooming glass flowers that wink in the sun.

Ragball

The knotted core
tied tightly with string,
then more plastic layers,
ribbons of banana palm,
sewn fabric patches,
like a sutured moon.

Shirtless children shouting *ballon;*
their deep brown skin
and hair with cherry highlights,
play as if starvation
was just a rumour.

They tire too soon,
those red flashes on their heads
is the flag of malnutrition,
and I loathe this ragball
that will last two generations.

GUILT

It is more difficult than you think,
        sitting in this lecture hall;
missing the snap of rounds
        that break the sound barrier.
Feeling tough with a shoulder slung
        Browning Hi-Power,
holding it out, looking at my armed shadow
        like Peter O'Toole's T.E. Lawrence.

Sunlight pressing against Chapel Bay,
        stones exhale at sunset.
Drifting to class,
        my contemplative not for *The Iliad*;
across the wine dark sea,
        my brothers are away at war.

I don't crave combat,
        am not blood thirsty,
but I do desire the experiences
        that my friends will suffer.
I imagine driving in the packet, waiting
        to erupt hot plates of shrapnel. On patrol,
little balls of compact razors
        that bounce up to explode at your pelvis.
IEDs that look like children's toys,
        explosive vests, worn by little boys.

That I am here and they are there
        stings of jealousy,
is worse than humiliation. Guilt
        for not going, when they share
their stories like Confession. Guilt,
        when I am relieved of a burden
that makes them so different.

Bara Ex Nihilo

We ran into the thunderstorm and your foot caught,
that osteoporotic femur snapped like a green branch:
You rolled over in the grass, half submerged in a puddle,
and cried out for a *fucking bucket*.
Then sang an endless masterpiece of profane phrases
into existence, until I brought the fucking bucket,
wondering why you didn't just barf on the grass.

Tipped it up over your head, like a
medieval knight about to joust;
the fingertips of rain—a tympani.
Grey felt clouds billowed from the lip
of the upturned pail, as you smoked a cigarette
in deafening solitude.

Chlorine Poseidon

Screaming obscenities under water
        to a chlorine Poseidon,
shaking his finger at competitors
        like a madman,
dunking his head in the pool
        on hands and knees
then spitting it back,
        as though to claim it for his own.

Insulted a drunk in a Montreal tavern
        and was killed on the street.
Our pure
        maple syrup Victor Davis;
kicking chairs
        in front of Her Majesty The Queen
and surging,
        like a speakeasy.

Sennacherib's Prism

Bully-bearded Assyrians
ride heavy sledges
in the killing fields outside Lachish;
they grind bodies into the earth;
a rude victory recorded
on Sennacherib's prism.

When they came for us,
our walls were tall.
We had spent years.
From the heights
we saw writhing fields of enemy.
Sang to *HaShem*,
sang the chorus together
so they'd know we couldn't
be defeated.

Cooled our mouths with well water,
stayed calm and broke bread,
opened jars of grain and olive oil,
waited, waved over the sun-hot walls,
spat date pits with wit;
allowed time to be our brother.

Stood and screamed,
pointed, cursed, piled sling stones
when they came close, burned them alive;
so many that our lamps were dark at night.
Drank skins of blood grape
as the moons flushed,
while our ally winds whipped the sand
like razors of truth.

Until one starless night
the sword of dysentery came to them whispering;
HaShem's angels callously walked through
their skin tents on the cull,
so our story in cuneiform
sings of resolve, not of trapped birds.

Ivy the Belly Dancer

My friend had similar size feet:
      I traded him sandals for shoes
so that I might walk
      the dark-haired dancer home.
It took me three streets
      to fall in love
as she moved through the veil of harbour fog.

She was going to school
      taking science courses,
and belly dancing,
      enjoying an immigrant social life
in our Canadian
      port side city.

Everything about her
      was intriguing;
like when she was in Egypt
      she learned how to sew sutures
by practicing on
      a torn leather armchair,
then was put to work
      in a Cairo hospital.

For the next few months
      we were inseparable,
our first passion
      penetrating The Citadel;
the way her olive skin
      contrasted mine,
how warm
      her body always was,
with jagged strips of hair
      painting sweat onto my chest.

She sent me a letter yesterday;
   exotically postmarked.
The short vague script
   of an acquaintance,
with a photograph,
   that I searched for detail,
and found
   Ivy forcing a smile
through the veil
   of her wedding dress.

Heard at Dave Mullally's Wake: Souris River PEI

Doc Mullally's box-sled broke through the ice,
the frozen sheet popping like taillights.
Unable to pull out the mare,
a Mountie ended the misery with his revolver.

She slid into hardening slush,
rolling like an iceberg,
her great rump rose above the waterline,
a frozen drumlin hardening like rock,
a bump, a horsehair bench, there all winter long,
lingering, a freezing of fates;
sat on, by the young people,
to tie up their skates.

THE PRESSBOARD BOX

Aproned women reeling in the line,
dropping wooden clothes pegs into a strawberry quart basket,
clattering like the bones of babies who died their first winter.

Homemade quilts being pulled in
like the cod nets and the jigging line;
work britches with their tapestry of patchwork,

twisting water out of fabric
under the scrutiny of two red squirrels
chattering impatiently in the damaged eaves;

waiting to perform their high-wire robbery
of the bird feeder that topped a pole slick with grease
and anchored that ran the clothesline.

We called those squirrels The Great Zucchinis:
Memory of an old pressboard box;
the one that the General Electric dryer came in.

We played in it as if it were our very own cave,
sometimes we were trapped in an avalanche,
or riding for our first time in the Dining Car of the CPR

It was a bank we robbed and a trench in The Great War
where we fought beside our grandfathers
in The Battle of the Somme

But we never hauled imaginary fish into our private haven
maybe we were more afraid than we knew
of the unanticipated rage of the ocean,

or the calloused stench of the hands,
or the fishhook scars that paid for the appliance,
in boatloads, of catches, in years.

SALAMATU

She wanders the supermarket
for the first time.
A metal cart on smooth lubricated wheels,
instead of a balanced wicker basket;
through the Byzantine labyrinth,
the flawless rows of aluminum tins
with their joyous faces,
etched like alabaster jars and bas-reliefs
from an ancient tomb.

Salamatu's cream palms reach into the air
and she's dancing;
swaying like the tops of trees,
hardly believing the size;
the enormous yields—
obelisks of canned food
for the inevitable drought.
Nobody starves here?
Not the sick. Not even the lazy.

Until
a sudden solemnity,
drops down like a machete,
she goes quiet,
barely able to contain the new burden—
there is an aisle in this labyrinth
for pets.

Grinling Gibbons aka Inigo Jones

If he carved them open,
he had been paid, and
brilliant pods illustrated
paid well.

His peas were open,
or closed,
were either copiously
split and bearing fruit,
or flat, without reward,
as empty ballet shoes
droop, without the
foot of a dancer, down
like the wrinkled face
of Old Walter,
after his stroke.

Gibbons chiselled ribbons,
picture frames
architectural flourishes
on pretty things
carved for kings
who now occupy space
in ossuaries—in his valley
of dry bones.

But there in the mantles,
above the cackle
of peat fires,
underneath mirrors,
in the margins, around
noble paintings, are the
souls of the carvers,
and every
pea pod is a poem.

SEA KING

An exhausted Sea King helicopter
running on petrol vapour and prayers
took a run at landing in the gale,
pausing above the teeter-totter deck
lifting and rolling in the swells,
radar mast slashing,
an aviator's Atlantic sword dance.

In this same winter wind,
the chickadees hovered helpless
as the wicked ice lashed the windows,
and the chimney banshee called,
as the house breathed heavy
in the merciless pulse of the storm.

Like a great frigate offering sanctuary
from the slicing winds
that moved in waves across the fields,
my lady opened the patio doors
and invited in the watch cap-wearing
chickadees.

The straw-boned birds
tap dance on her palm,
eating sunflower seeds that
have been husked with her teeth,
like Saint Francis; she is the saviour ship,
where we can descend, the chickadees and I,
flagging crewmen, saved from a fall
to the black ice-strewn waters
of a lonely ocean.

Temptress

She came slurring out of darkness
toward the campfires, under grey plank piers
with duel citizenship, adulterated accent,
wearing Fimo necklaces, flashes of lapis
lazuli, long hair tied with woven cords
and knowledge of our passwords.

We were hauling fishing nets, wet ropes
and the hopes that younger men shoulder;
juxtaposed with the hollow sorrows
of our mirrors, before the miles;
into eyes that rarely cry
whilst we shave 'round forced smiles.

When she sang the men sat forward
and ignored our own jealous women.
The waves surged with the urge to come closer,
in the way that danger seems like praise to boredom.
I could hear the crashing, that sounded like applause
against the Causeway to Cape Breton.

Lured by attractive chances,
the winds played witching refrains
with the leaves and through the branches.
She stumbled over the moonbeam's snare
staggered through the fire between our chairs,
tread on my sleeping guitar case.

Morning's mist, the sun splintered through,
there on the edge of our fire-pit, in the powder ash,
a smooth dragline as from rope, and stranger marks
where she'd spun in circles and tripped
onto the face of the instrument's sarcophagus—
leaving faint, cloven, hoof-prints.

Elvira, Mistress of the Dark

Tidewater kiss onto black lipstick,
      mistress.
Thank you
      for introducing
            Boris Karloff;

Important to meet
      Arthur Conan Doyle.
A black tied up affair;
      match your provocative
            evening gown,

cut into
      midnight.

All the credit is not yours entirely,
my insomnia receives some of the glory
      for our sojourns together;
when you teased me
      with
            your witching,

power,
      sexuality.

I would meet more women with your charms;
have painted nails
      rake blood from my back.
but you were the first;

wearing good and evil like a theme,
with surface tension,
      your ready bosom
           holding,

gliding hips,
        a moistened treble clef,
your lips,
        like Eden's apple.

Barber Shop Prophets

Pinaud Clubman talc
is whisked onto the neck like crop dust,
from oil cans that sing a tin melody
as they are played by scholarly thumbs.

Somewhere upon a ledge
you see a graduated glass cylinder,
cobalt blue, like a monochrome summer sky,
or the venous blood, and clear as a dead lake;
70's wallpaper tattered and tobacco streaked;
hickory walking canes, leaning,
dead flies supine on the windowsill of their eternity.

Sitting like the subject of a Norman Rockwell painting,
straight razor held to you with hands that could perform surgery,
rigid on the chair, as if seeing a new fawn frozen against
the backdrop of a wheat field.

Burnt offerings;
cherry and vanilla pipe smoke.
There is sanctification.
It will wash over you, will purify.
Develop an ear for the strands of wisdom;
remember their stories.
This is the language of the past;
cave paintings, totems, creation myth.

Admire the cadence of the scissors, soothsayers,
lovely whispers, like the eternal tides
of wind against bow bending cornrow.
The outside world distorted through century-glass;
imagine Plato's cave.
Speak less than you listen.
Always get the shave.

At Oxford

Under this Doric arch,
through a Gothic window
in Christ Church Cathedral,
the hallway of her body is adorned
with the painting of a king on horseback,
and seven queens staring out nervously.

Feel my way through her victory arch,
the hallway of her thighs
like an English sunrise,
thirsting for garden dew,
that spreads over landscape,
licks the sundial.

The ghosts of better men
have waltzed through these rooms.
Feel honoured, to have
been accepted to this edgy fraternity.

Paint my portrait so that others may compare
our styles of dress, their powdered hair; bow ties,
the fashion of a fanciful cuff, a scholarly scarf.
I have a place in her graceful echoes;
my portrait will be easy to spot,
as I'll be the only one grinning madly.

Requiem to the Karma Cat
Dedicated to the person who spray-painted "Phony Karma" all over Hamilton, Ontario

Aboard a city bus
      crossing the MacDonald Bridge,
Dartmouth to Halifax, back bench.

The bumper stickers of the trailing pickup,
"Enjoy Canadian lamb, twenty thousand
      coyotes can't be wrong."
"Life isn't for fun, life is for working,
      fear the Devil, and soon you'll be gone."

Two university age girls
      speaking Yiddish, "Shayna Punim."
Buddhist's rub standard white Jesus
      on the belly for luck.
A poster above the trip-wire,
      the ding of a bell,
"Pregnancy, need help, call us,
      free and confidential."

Illuminated letters, on the back of the seat,
      as if painted by a monk.
"I want to fuck your mother."
      Taking out my pen I responded,
"Dad, go home,
      you're drunk."

Odd that I should respond, at my age,
      a passenger above the Halifax Harbour,
where Irving oil tankers
      can vandalize the water.

Perhaps it was like Mozart's wife, who would play
      all but the last note to get him out of bed,
so that he would have to plunk the final chord,
      to complete the uncompleted.

This is for you Karma Cat, who wrote
      "Phony Karma" on everything in Hamilton;
on liquor store windows, in phone booths, around telephone poles,
      on bridges over the QEW, even the Escarpment got it.
Street writer Laureate,
      virtuoso of paint-can,
I'll hoist one to you, from on this bus,
      to the greatest poet of all,
      Anonymous.

Tragedy, Ruah and Whiskey
For Fast Eddie Legere

A black flag has been raised above the theatre
there it snaps concealed outrage
in the surges, like a blacksmith's hearth
heavy on the bellows,
chattering like a dark crow
or a prophet who issues warning.

The rise and fall;
playing their dangerous melody
on sad violins. With tightened bows
the resin drifts
onto thin fabric
defenceless against enemy winds.

With his pants falling down
stained, stenched, whiskered, whiskied, bent—
Eddie the Bum staggered down centre stage.
A car stopped on Main Street, Crown lawyer jogged over
took his own belt off, looped it through Eddie's pants
and pulled them up for him.

Fast Eddie was thrown into jail before pneumonia season,
for warm Richibucto cells, soft cots, screws who smile.
Moncton's Judges will act as pallbearers; who
once gave him an extra week of jail time, at Eddie's request
so that he could enjoy Christmas meal, and fruit cake,
and mumble about the open air hockey games.

Happiness came in the daubs of pitch between the planks,
his life was the cracks within timber; his last breath
a stirring final tragic soliloquy—but it seemed
that he fell on his sword in almost every scene,
tumbling over lines echoed in tragic chorus.

The ropes slap against the tall oaken pole, take notice—
it has been there a lifetime.
A black flag has been raised above the theatre,
the exhaled spirit profanely scolding, somehow standing
taller in death, forgiving us our trespasses.

MAY I USE YOU AS A REFERENCE?
For Samps

Like university freshmen,
leaning from car windows,
his roses—the ones he couldn't peddle
last night in the barrooms—
looked defeated, facing the floor
with their drooping melancholy.

But his flower-selling days were over now—
His liver had surrendered.
This Gottingen Street boarding room was a tin-can graveyard,
like an anarchistic Warhol painting—
in the smoldering murk of Campbell's soup ashtrays.

A dancing Holstein sleeping bag
was strangling a Gonorrhea-stained mattress.

His tuxedo jacket had given up,
its arms folded in resignation on the floor,
as if to say, my dance card's full daddy,
find me another job.

He took a slug from a naked silver beaker,
stripped from the fascist paper label,
and took a hot whiskey shit.
He used a chipped enamel pot to top-up
the holding tank for a rare flush—
Pondered a shave, and the update of his resume.

Moonlight upon my Muse

Repeating perfect lines without speaking
Taking the skin off in a solitary ribbon,
like circling with the harrow
Passing each plump wedge from fingerprints
Where juice runs downhill to fill liquid undulations
Of a tilled field, whose horizontal lines accept rainwater and
hold topsoil

A prairie of Christmas tangerines in a balsam wood crate
Floating into the ionosphere, where honest lips tighten
As a new moon leans into a blackening sky
Supinating against night, remembering dash-lit smiles
On coastline drives through darkness

Beside a silver pathway written over the Bay of Fundy
Drawing a line between the thin slice of the moon to her eyes
Clearly ordained, constellations obey the Maker
As if the heavens have been instructed, this night
To keep the spotlight on her

Atop the Downs

Under this bright definition
of a full moon,
chattering sheep call to us
like landscape angels.

Thirteen of us,
four men, nine women
walk delicately through darkness
over five thousand year old foundations.

Complex community ritual,
earthen ramparts still visible,
mysteries undisclosed,
fire wastes deep within, flickering
secrets, ramparts, and berm.

Dancing barefoot upon
a Neolithic burial barrow.

We stand naturally, celestial circle,
four choose to remove clothing,
bathing in smooth blue light—
Dark areolas, nipples erect;
join hands; lean back into stars
breasts crested,

with the panorama
of pin-bright villages
stretching away
from the White Sheet Downs.
We sing,
women's voices seize the night;
inspired harmonies,
union.

Closer now,
whispering together,
in prayer,
honest timber in voices,
dripping with honeyed worthiness.

Undisclosed ancient understanding,
underfoot,
within the ground,
deep within ourselves.

So different from daytime disguises
or the lies they tell each other;
rehearsed religious passwords
and automatic pious phrases.

This moment holds more truth
than a thousand churches;
God's honesty is here
under these stars
and can be navigated by moonlit smiles.

Prime Minister Macbeth

The House of Commons
has been a churning cauldron,
with three haggish sisters
stirring sinister ingredients;
adding wing of bat separatism,
Grit foetus ripped from womb.

Senators and gargoyles grin madly
from parliamentary perches,
hissing wildly
under the silvery moon.

Run from the naughty worms,
scream for Aboriginal rights,
when will our fishing nets
dance the saltwater two-step,
or softwood lumber's
ransom lay?

Let Lady Beef be
drawn and quartered,
and working women
fair pay.

Poets to the Menin Gate

The Northern Salient is a loam ossuary
crested with golden fields of Trappist Abbey hops
sunken bones and unexploded shells,
woven with thin roads,
Tyne Cott's numbered stones,
Sanctuary Wood,
Ieper's cathedral bells.

Listen to the whispers,
Wilfred Owen's moaning orison,
the nightmare madness of Sassoon,
cruel April's chlorine creeping.
The names written on the Menin Gate,
once thick-pocked and septic stench,
the hollow horns weeping.

Forever wounded souls,
drowning infanteers,
blinded by the searing gas,
roped together like climbers.
Led to the rear.
Sweet-smelling Poperinge nurses
gave morphine to deafen the pain.

Distance from the murd'rous howls,
we are left to read their verses,
of the battlefield's terrible cries,
and the poet-soldier's curses.

War

He's filmed it before, war
Took pictures of gore,
Firefight-love, adrenaline high, war
Lost his brethren, learned to hate,
Hated their differences, feared, war
Saw smiling children,
Killed a family in a car, war
Ignored someone's torture,
Mercy-shot a wounded Taliban fighter, war
Lied about his work,
Held rage like an IED, war
Drank too much to forget,
Hit his wife, cut her lip, war
Not the friend I knew before.

Dead Fly

Everything in the Halifax Armouries
needed to be labeled, and accounted for.
A plastic ribbon, the title, a stencil reference number
logistical knots, legions of documents, ligatures
of signatures—forms filled in triplicate.
Extra-terrestrial beings will look at these pages
in some future century and say,
this is what they killed the trees for.

Deny the reason behind an action,
like some bursting supernova of cognitive dissonance
that our names of things will live on in the supernatural
cartouches of time.

Like the racehorse with blinders, so they
don't jump at every fencepost shadow,
something in their prehistoric genes tells
them to leap over the thin dark cracks so you
won't break your momma's back.

Pound your boot nails down. Step on the cracks—take
the shortcuts, or one day, you will look up on your
pregnant file cabinets and recognize that
Sergeant MacFarlane has taken absurdity
into the realm of the metaphysical.
For there is a label there, a stencil beside a corpse.
#01—DEAD FLY

THE SEAHORSE TAVERN

Halifax's oldest vinegar house
her distressed timber pub sign
with jaundice seahorse crest,
moved indoors.
Descending wide cathedral stairs
to the glorious sour cellar.

The sign, retired from beckoning
bleary-eyed patrons
the faded emblem's sandy
crimson chain,
bleeds time against stale brick,
perspiring rust into thirsting mortar

like a concave shield
that rests proudly in alcove
or above mantle, in the darkening:
Standing the watch between
the sunset of youth,
and ghosts unseen.

The Banker on the Unicycle

There is a former magician on Bay Street
      riding his unicycle toward the giant institutions;
in his freedom above the herds of Torontonians
      he glides, stops sharp, quickly back pedals,
changes his direction twenty, now forty degrees,
      to pass a blind man tap tap tapping;
who hears the slight creak of metal
      like a bicycle,
so he tenses and collects his shoulders,
      but the magician is past him;

maintaining the rhythm, the pendulum,
      balancing like Platonic justice,
standing out in the collage of heads and hats,
      like a Hamilton smokestack,
writing progress in long drags
      that ash into our Great Lakes.

He has fallen before
      like Icarus to the grey blacktop,
to the delight of the Samaritan masses
      who helped him to his feet, smirking,
because everyone likes to see
      blood on the knee
and the torn suit,
      of a banker on Bay Street.

Rugby

He took the hit under his smooth
chin, his head snapped up
as he fell back onto his heels, balanced
for an eternity,
then tumbled, as if the body were
an empty suit of armour,
clattering to the field;

the only time I've run onto the pitch
to hear him breathing unnaturally quick,
within the heavy shroud of a seizure;
face down; I joined him,
our bodies in a line,
I placed my palms against his ears
and held his spine still while
he twitched and trembled.

The sirens, the spine-board, the
Off-duty nurses, his curses when
he awoke and couldn't feel
his legs, the dregs of his teenage
days, belayed and hanging
in the fear of tomorrow.

THE GIRLS DOOR

Downwind from a memory
    the mulberry tree
        and sweet grasses.

Dancing moon, shy moon,
    shifting frozen, keeping time,
        ellipse sky, an oblate millwheel.

Behind Father Loftus School,
    dipping cattails into kerosene,
        blazing torches touch crisp air;

holding glowing dandelions
    as temporary as fireworks,
        burning out like stars;

casting wilderness shadows,
    onto brick cornerstone,
        illuminating arches,

under the Girls entrance,
    where we have come this night,
        like so many other nights

to spill together
    as light and shadow share spaces,
        linger for a while,

downwind from a memory,
    the mulberry tree,
        and sweet grasses.

SHANNON'S STILL LIFE

I was sitting at the Trident Booksellers and Café
when I overheard, "Those date squares are supposed
to be cut into rectangles."
Outside a pigeon was landing
on a pastel canvas awning,
a man was yawning, he came in
passing a red-haired girl with a nose-ring
with "Shannon" written
on her clothes tags.

There is a thin scar on the back of her neck,
like a comet's cut across the sky,
so perfect in direction,
my tattoo in contrast;
a lack of truth stamped there
unlike her wound, believed, through accident achieved
left like a baby on steps,
so lovingly taken in, now belongs,
like magic that just happens,
and voices made for song.

My mark premeditated, thought out for at least
all of my life;
that comet comes to her honestly,
by circumstance,
caught on the nail of a porch, or maybe
made with the edge of a knife.

The comet passes to capture a moment along a line;
the mind's still life painting;
like preserved salamanders, pickled in formaldehyde.
Within the smells of the cafe and old books
I wondered
Could she love me?
Would we give each other scars
like the scuffs of character
etched into the black leather of her boots?

A proper blemish, like the smudge of a date rectangle
or lipstick, touched to Shannon's scarf.

I wished that I had known her all her life,
and so shared her childhood years:
That I could have been there the day
her comet caused her tears.

WE NEVER SEE THE TROLLS

In the archives
       of the Bodleian Library,
they work endlessly

locating this obscure text
       and that
Eliot's letters,
       Field Marshal Montgomery's memoirs.

Pulling our demands
       from the stacks,
sending them up to the light of man,
       on ancient cable elevators.

The smell of books
       that creak like progress,
their straining forearms,
       our viscous paper cuts.

Alas, these trolls
       are getting older,
their beards hang over
       plump bellies.

Some remember
       when the pillar stalactites
were just minerals dripping,
       salt for licking.

They still hope
       that one day humanity
will finally understand.

And they'll rise again
       from the catacombs
like wisdom literature.

For now, they continue
       tirelessly piling knowledge
onto rickety
       wooden carts,

oiling cable,
       maintaining the system
              mixing vats of glue;
we never see the trolls
       because they don't want us to.

They, in their cavernous subterfuge,
       occasionally debating if we have learned enough;
wondering when we'll be ready.

58

The Quality of Attention

Reigate lies inside the North Downs
like a contented lover.

Morning tea is served
outside my bedroom door.

Accompanied by her lingering musk;
a scented melody of the glorious

Austrian housekeeper,
in clever concord with nature.

O cruel nature!
Dances her twenty years away.

From my first poems about women,
young enough to be her grandchildren.

Cheerily walk through grey evening fog,
Down the blue moonlit field path,

to the glowing beacon of pub-song, where
David Halliwell, the playwright, holds court.

> The scenery: hearth and half-timber
> The plot: driven by character

Successful dialogue, he explains,
does not materialize from how well you write

but from how well you listen; it is achieved
through quality of attention.

I take a piss and notice that the condom machine
Dispenses lemon drops.

Theme: metamorphosis

Conversation turns back to the glorious housekeeper,
whose Viennese accent sings,

like realistically sly dialogue—the ale taps turn away,
embarrassed,

like the necks of great birds, the Queen's royal geese,
ashamed of the colonial and the drunk playwright,

who talk of their forbidden chambermaid, cursing
the chasms of time between them and her;

one longing to be twenty years younger,
the other, twenty years older.

Courtly Love

She bakes me lemon bread
Sings softly to newborn children
Wears flowers upon her head
Nature smiles free from burden

Gently milks the kine at sunrise
Pours cool water of jealous embers
Where honesty in her children's eyes
Pours forth tears of joy from silver rivers

When she comes into a room
Poets write with shaking hand
The painters ache, musicians tune
Philosophes try to understand

I pray the Lord will collect my soul
A melancholy I could not endure
When our village church bells toll
The first day we are without her

Lord of Heaven, when her star fades
When West Wind blows asunder
Let Angel's weep, like newborn sheep
For a world alone, in pain, in wonder

MY FIRST PROTEST—A SNOW ANGEL

The husks of wild grape remnants,
        vines clinging to a wire paddock fence;
grey posts wearing
        milk whit bowler hats of snow,
like tiny drumlins of albino coal dust
        piled for a frigid hearth.

The winter after the barn caught fire,
        remember the ornate wicker angel
cresting our scotch-pine,
        my boomerang waiting underneath the boughs,
wrapped in
        Christmas tissue.

Snow boots with felt-liners
        coming back from the pond
in the far field,
        windswept terra-firma;
deep drifts to smuggle my body through,
        pushing on, face stinging in the wind.

My older sister ahead,
        annoyed with my slow progress;
angry when I could not keep up
        in the burning cold,
complaining, and feeling deserted,
        I called out for her.

She now claims,
        as we sit round the kitchen table thirty years later,
that she was trying to inspire me
        when she called me a whining asshole.
I laid down defiantly in the snow,
        fanned my arms and legs,
and pissed in my snowsuit.

ONE STONE

I once chose the perfect flat stone
skipped it once, twice, thrice—
over the glass smooth lake,
in a flourish of ripple rings
collapsing against each other, then,
plunging through thin layered depths to darkness,
descending into the shifting currents of time
and the mythology of former lovers.

She has whispered every secret to me,
of the suitors and simple men
whom she has ridden, then discarded;
waiting for the great Odysseus to return.

Examined each for quality,
for usefulness,
then slung them through the air,
to watch them dance atop a liquid mirror,
reflecting the churning eternal sky,
tapping across water like wingtips,
for two or three beautiful ricochets.

Before they flew from her hand,
before the dead cold bottom darkness,
she must have carefully felt each one,
made earnest love to their differences,
searched for a water smooth stone,
with a perfect character, a dangerous weight,
like David, preparing his sling for a bloodletting.

SYRINGE ROBBERY

Urine yellow stained Hypodermic plastic,
infused residue of crack cocaine
and vinegar, then hit to the vein,
to the swirling beauty of smooth metal windmills
oscillating on distant hills,
their sleek blades like Spitfire propellers.

Until the inevitable winding down
and a kid at an all-night gas station, then
to all night corner store.
Weeping sores. Armed with a syringe.

Clutching the scores in a fist
like The Internationale,
folding away on a stolen bicycle
through Moncton's midsummer rain;
ten-speed clicking. Sorrow pedaling past
on a binge-ride to nowhere.

At the bridge, with thirsty syringe,
sluggish, sleepy-eyed droplets glinting,
spitting then high.
A frog choir is boasting to the supermoon,
saltwater tides rise, chocolate riverside
cracked like elephant skin. She's thin,
arms and legs pockmarked lunar landscapes.

The RCMP see the bicycle reflector,
arrest her beside the river;
in court, her blood is considered a lethal weapon,
another emotionless mug-shot—
a thirteen-month prison sentence.

To My Future Wife

Who could still my pen with a whisper
or part my veins with a word

FARMER WAITING IN THE BANK

A man in a checkered shirt and a Co-op hat
squeezes the polyester leaf of an artificial Boston ivy.
A difficult summer, too much damn rain.
Even the cylindrical baler couldn't save the hay
from the drowning.
Now the plastic plant inside the bank whispers,
"They are going to foreclose."

What the fuck do they know of the blood
that runs into the soil,
or the dancing cows licking fermented grain
at the base of the silo?
All of our children rode in the bucket
of the Massey-Harris. Danny drove it to graduation.

What do they know of sunsets behind crops,
of Hide-and-Seek in tall corn,
or the three-holed outdoor shitter?
They wear Sunday pants, decorate with plastic
plants.

Teenage Girl I Know

Fresh page-white purity,
swaddling clothes,
a princess wedding,
the family tree.
Winter's bedding.
Balancing on
brittle branches.

As white as the bleach marks
from the time she tried
to wash her clothes drunk.
Skin tight blue jeans,
knees frayed.

Menstruation and spilled wine,
a cancelled road trip,
clear-cut floodplains,
asbestos-lined pipes,
coughing children,
bleeding lungs,
tattoos and pink lipstick,
the piercing of the tongues.

The entire world's a sinkhole,
crash of her first car,
abortion, distortion,
the addition of a scar.
Self-obsession, self-doubt,
she's cutting.

Sleeping on strange floors,
to learn so many lessons,
boys who open doors,
the first sexual sessions.
Guarding father watching
at the window.
Fear and hatred and war,
realizing one day that her truth
is not his truth anymore.

Maine Snowfall

Mountains of metaphors
Spoken with a New England accent
As comfortable as distant sleigh bells
That dance for a moment on the tongue

Like an intricate snowfall
Where one flake melts into the body
To be spat from an iron bridge above grey water
Or left on the soft abdomen of a naked woman

Ingested through the breast
Taken from the swelling nipple
Or drips through membrane
And is drawn over desirable curves

A dampness that passes between us
Having been carried through me
To be purified in you

BANANA PANCAKES

I remember the saltwater taste
as I kissed her shoulders while she slept;
her tanned body penetrating the night
with heat radiating from our sunburns;

her eyes fluttered open in the cool breeze of morning;
she asked for banana pancakes and oral sex,
which I gave her—
not in that order;

when she came I heard a loon's spiralling cry
cast across the quiet lake;
acknowledging how good it was to be married,
to the only other couple within hollering distance.

WHEN DO YOU HUG A MOUNTIE?

When do you hug a Mountie? Never—
unless you're from Moncton—
after three have crossed the river—
when tears have rained, unrestrained,
the city, a lockdown nightmare.

You never hug a Mountie, unless
their blood is tunic red, apply a tourniquet,
add pressure, more than you think necessary.
Wait for the sirens, while grade school kids
hold onto their handlebars
and look up the road toward eternity,
where help will come,
but you never hug a Mountie
unless you're from Moncton.

You never should hug a Mountie,
but you may hug their widows,
hug their dog-eyed fatherless children
all you like. Hug them every day,
with scholarships or groceries.
Do hug their families ten years down the road,
when the landscaping is overrun,
and the driveways are cracked
in the unforeseeable, hollows, of time.

Humanism

She calls me a Renaissance man
Because I write poems I guess
And coos when I wear my reading glasses

She has a real penchant for footwear
Her gallant accoutrements
Singing out to manicured feet

Teasingly claims that her feet are the greatest
And that mine are ugly, with scars, from stitches .
As if sexuality were bound in sandal and boot alone

Her gait is saintly
The church fathers follow her with glazed eyes
Wishing for a moment that they were me

LOVE LETTER TO A SOLDIER

When he unrolled his sock-donuts
a tiny note tickertaped to the floor
of our canvas tent.

In the pulsing kerosene light
he read her script, then held it
underneath his moustache, to breathe in
what she had left him there.

I recalled how Sir Walter Raleigh
cut a love letter into glass with
a diamond.

One soldier I know had one written
on rose petals, sewn carefully together
with his lover's hair.

There, in the hot whisper of gaslight,
they were dancing. For an instant
the tent was a soft moss forest floor
where the picnic basket rests, and the
waterfalls drone white noise to the
entwined lovers, resting on their home-made quilt.

In that blessed *analepsis* he was away
from the business of painting targets
with lasers, from insurgents, drone strikes,
IED casualties, ramp ceremonies.

Away from the bagpipe requiems below the tail
of the C-130 Hercules,
and the long funerary drive on Canadian highways,
under frowning flag draped bridges,
to the equally long and lonely symptoms
of PTSD.

In that tent he was himself, with her, before
the sandstorms of war, and the digging out.

BELFAST

A pack of children ricochet
against the Falls Road
like rubber bullets.
Slap silver spectacles
off the face of a woman.
Flat handed strike,
like a tipper to a bodhran.
A leering tourist
admiring giant murals,
funeral-faced hunger strikers.

Ransom snatched up,
artful dodgers scatter
like laughter
between their tenements.
One lonely-eyed boy
freckled, wild Irish hair
returns her wire-rims,
head bowed, in offering,
with gentle hands.
Then turns
like a startled pheasant,
thrumming back
to the loyal brethren
of Ulster.

WAY TOO MUCH TO DRINK

The magazine holds ten
golden promises
manacled one above the other;
when slid neatly into the black handle;
it makes a metallic sigh.
The cylinder is cool on my brow. Looking
into the dark tunnel, that can speak
like Cordelia.

The hammer is a clitoris that pulses
under my thumb,
as I slip one finger slowly
past the guard into the crescent.

There is a scar on my index finger
where I feel nothing; beside it,
flesh with nerve endings that radiate,
a purposeful twitch
toward a death scene
that I can write across this bedroom.

NASON
For Trevor Nason (1984–2011)

I'm drinking whiskey
from your laboratory beaker
something you'd never done
preferring instead to get high
on Jesus,
motorcycles, and
making students laugh.

Your science class
was a stand-up routine
complete with fizzing pyrotechnics
that popped and hissed and
taunted school smoke alarms.
Endothermic reactions
were sexier than sex.

The mural they painted
outside your room
was pure catharsis,
a vision of you
walking in your blue lab coat,
drinking coffee from
a four hundred ml beaker.

I remember your catch phrase:
Knowledge is half the battle;
the other half is laser beams.
I remember the girl who
cut her wrists.
You told her that she was having
a bad day,
not a bad life, and
she believed you.

THE FIST-FIGHT ON POETRY NIGHT
for Steve Hay

Three poets pouring, pouring out their souls
Three barmaids pulling, pulling on their taps
One noisy patron, pissing out his prose
Disrupting the reading, breaking the nose
One Scottish actor, urging a patron to be still
That patron rising, threatening-threatening-threats

The setting down of pints, the taking up of fists
The drawing of the daggers, the glinting of their tips
One poet wades in; breaking arm and chair
Adjusting their temper, with Wilde-wine eyed-flare
His arms now open, like the cross of a kite
Or a Christ who's come a-rumblin', on Poetry Night

Three poets pouring, pouring out their souls
Three barmaids pulling, holy water from their taps
That quiet patron, listening in repose
One Scottish actor, waiting for his chance

Scissors in Grade Three

Thumb and
three finger
Trigger guards
Manufacture snowflakes
Assembly line style
Smooth plump hearts
One for every
Potential future wife
Fourteen girls
And an extra one
For Teacher

THE MYSTERY OF TEENAGERS

The students groan in Gregorian unison,
slandering their humble teacher's joke before it can root;
his words refract off their super-cool personas
or crash-land like wounded seabirds.
They all hunt the albatross.
Even when he uses pyrotechnics
or defeats gravity by levitation, they yawn. Not the
polite, discreet yawns either; but bold in-yer-face
you're-boring-me-to-death yawns.

Somehow, they make friends with their head-phones on
between hot pepper texting and tweets,
their diets are unbalanced,
they'd never eat pickled beets: No time for preserves, man.

They won't believe their days are numbered
their heady adventures counted and culled,
but they make his life the dregs worth drinking,
they show him that the mete and dole of living
is living young.

A Prayer for Cold Hands

My tight cold fist pummeled your beautiful face
because you had stolen my mittens.
Proud to have stood against injustice,
I boasted to my father about the copious nosebleed,
how I dissected your hands, your surprise
when I snapped you with a calibrated left.
Sapphire eyes spoke of an immeasurable loss
that would take me years to understand.

That night Dad, appalled, tore me out,
from soft eiderdown quilts.
We drove past the Ancaster Heights
under one radiant star,
past the triple rinks to the end of the *H.S.R.
Stopped in front of a dying farmhouse.

Imploding timbers leaned sick,
scratching rat decay, damp lagging
nested with pregnant cats
behind greased tarpaulin and potato sacks.
Your hungry brothers and sister lay in half-sleep.
I ached with shame. Dad stepped out,
quietly kicked off his work boots.

In stocking feet he crossed your porch
depositing a basket of preserves, Mom's bread,
maple fudge and an envelope.
Covered the basket with a familiar iron wash basin,
weighed it down with a brick, stole back
to where I waited.
We did not talk on the ride home
teaching the type of anonymous giving
that never happens in a poem.

The next morning I returned the mittens,
offering hat and scarf, shoes, a pair of green wellies.
You said that you forgave me
but your eyes could not.

Give me the wisdom to know
when to keep my hands at my side,
give me the courage to know
when and from whom to raise them,
and to forever, to forever,
let my hands be cold.   *Hamilton Street Railway

THE SUBSCRIPTION

We argue as if we are driving
on an endless rotary;
she told me to love her like Petrarch,
put a limit on drinking, excommunicated cigars,
then ordered me a one year fitness magazine subscription.

It arrived in a fortnight, shrink-wrapped
with scores of chickpea recipes.
She opened it first and was horrified
at the sculpted Aphrodite that caressed the glossy pages;
plump with pouting athletic poise,
pulsing pink lunged musculature, trim
tanned and jangly—wearing make-up
and the dusted perfection of an air brush edit, crop, and reduction.

She cut them out. Windowed my pages leaving the
hairless male weightlifters and artichoke articles.
Censored photos of the women, as if it were a *Hustler*.

The next month I got to it first; and cut out those flexing sirens,
smiling mischievous centrefolds.
I taped this harem everywhere: supine under her pillow,
buxom behind the teacups, seraphim smiling in the freezer,
mascara eyes hinting of mystery on the toiled lid,
with a few rolled into the toilet paper scroll
to emerge, streaming into her life
like the parchment of former lovers.

ABOUT HIS STUDENT'S AGE

Their teacher in bow tie
with thin tweed shoulders twitching,
reacting with every school bell; the ring
causing uncontrollable jerkiness.

Only years before, pulling the hollow Lee Enfield trigger,
303 brass tumbling into the blood and muck,
rattling off the duckboards
in the zig-zag trench lines of Belgium.

Loud noise brought him to Passchendaele,
to the mudscape of an A.Y. Jackson canvass;
an eviscerated horse hanging in the scorched branches,
the lonesome tree a church.

Twining trenches canopied with stars,
close shells screaming like Dante's tormented eternity,
distant guns double-thump, a panorama of explosives
pulsing orange and red like heat lightning.

Harassing fire, sleeplessness, rats and wet,
little bugs that bit, crotch rot, sewer soup,
back to the ruined farmlands of his Northern Salient,
every time a textbook hit a table.

Schoolgirls had taken interest in his facial tics,
and convinced their classmates to pound down their hardcovers
sending him shell shocked over the top,
back to the last day of his youth;

to the execution pole in Poperinge,
where he lined up in a row of twelve
and following orders, shot one his own;
a teenage boy, for running.

LAST OUT OF THE INNING

The rosin bag dropped to the lee of the hill
sticky fingers spinning seams of Braille.

From the top of the chest plate across the buckle
throwing high-heat, a curve, or a knuckle.

He reads flash-finger signals, like dancing legs,
inside the squatting shin-pad Proscenium.

With a nod, the batter guesses a curve on the edge
a dirt rainbow for swingers who just can't resist,

the large serving of cutters and sins,
or high and inside as the music of chins.

With the threat of a steal the pitcher looks over,
the fielders are back to the edge of the clover.

The clack of a slingshot's marble against picket,
crepuscular rays, through the web of his mitt,

spit in the glove that's well worn,
a can of corn.

CROWS

Nefarious crow, a horse barn arsonist,
carrying a cigarette dog-end, up into the mow.

They gather in the malignant hundreds,
become dark keyholes in the trees,

beside the wet highway scars, where cars crumple
into ditches like abandoned poems.

Indifferent and eerily quiet in the grey gloaming,
silent voyeurs in the nakedness of winter.

Soon, on the ground, like crooked old men,
they dance around a field mole, harvested from snow.

They beak it apart, circle-stab like Caesar
in a cacophony of barking.

Satisfied with the slip of a scalpel, or a cancerous
division of a cell; approving watchmen above

his duct tape tracheotomy; squirming through
the idling station wagon's window.

Playing Chess with Mohammed

Inside the Bodleian Library I'm on a laptop computer,
Wifi connection with Mohammed—we're playing chess;

our fifth match. He's a Sunni baker from Baghdad,
blistering samoon on the smooth stone oven,

protects the heart of the board with his knights
like Saladin.

This morning I heard the stuttering helicopters
from Hereford, flying umbrellas that protect the B52s,

rumbling away in long slow slants and shaking
the world, gorged and distended metal bomb bellies.

I text him, that in a few hours, the planes
will arrive. That he should get underground.

Before he clicks away, he offers a blessing; says
that he prays for me, that his daughter knows my name,

that Allah knows my name.

STEVEDORES

Stevedores unloading cathedral corridors,
of harbour front hardcovers,
shipping container spines, spires of cable cranes
standing atop the pier like bookends.
Loading docs, a Lego landscape,
where CN tracks suture oiled rocks,
where train cars collide and lock,
where foghorns howl across holy waters,
dip the dabbling fowl, where ships are christened,
with rhythmic engines chanting
the small tugs say rosaries
above the zebra mussel stowaways
on hulls, the gulls wheel through the high angle cable
restless for shift change and shore leave;
and when the paychecks arrive
the publicans get their tithes.

ONEIDA SCHOOLBOYS

Even our pencil crayons are racist;
the pink labelled *Flesh*

the brown crimson—*Indian Red*.
Bricks were made from clay, on sight,

where the Great Mother patted
her hand.

Above broken treaty hectares,
the hum of overhead projectors—

we make shadow wolves and hawks
against the drop down screens;

the whir like a distant waterfall.
In that tin box we hear ancestors

singing from eternity.
All the teachers are white.

Our classes have labels: *Basic* or *General Level*.
The flesh coloured kids take *Advanced* courses.

We never dance, we never drum,
but we roll our own tightly, and come undone.

LAST NAME

He arced the slender oak branch down;
pinned it under a rock,

two centuries later, at this bifurcation,
a peculiar elbow emerges from the trunk.

Roots are a ribcage that wrap around
the edge of the footpath,

or a bony hand reaching over the lip
of the escarpment, marking it.

Below, a cave opening, where fire starters
have tapped flint

to fry cattail and hickory bannock.
Then rest on smooth doeskin hides,

under mulberry ink drawings,
rock carvings, and names.

Four generations of your family sleep
against these walls in the layer of soapstone,

in this secret ossuary of memory. That too
is all about to die, my son.

Here, Finley, take this awl and scratch your name
below mine. Look, your aunt's name is there too;

who was taken when I was a boy.
I came here to cry and dream her back to life,

remembering that beautiful dark loneliness
that I was too young to understand.

You will be the last, before the earthmovers,
before the shape shifters come here to dig;

Caterpillars and track loaders will collapse
our secret cave; cannibalize this beauty for a box mall.

A café will overlook this waterfall. White noise,
white people;

where a chain-store will have the temerity
to sell dreamcatchers.

HAMILTON

Remember in the eighties when the scabs crossed our lines
Rolling the gauntlet of our picket we tossed barbs under the tires
They drove on rims for their sins, we caved their windshields in
More scared of mortgages than anything we did

Looking for just a little more, I'd like to see you come through
Looking for just a little more than what I was born to

The Hilton Works so full of jerks, strap the steel coils and wire
Sometimes I wake in molten glow and tearing of the fires
A cylinder went in the oxygen vessel, here, finish your glass of rye
Kept them alive just long enough for their wives to say goodbye

Looking for just a little more, I'd like to see you come through
Looking for just a little more than what I was born to

I'd walk the fence on my way to school, past the Camco
welding plant
During Vietnam did they build the bombs that we sent?
Stained glass windows and creaky stairs in my Aberdeen
apartment
Meeting Jenny under the overpass in the shadow of the
escarpment

Looking for just a little more, I'd like to see you come through
Looking for just a little more than what I was born to

Mise en abyme

I won't be paying money
for this ride.

Their zeitgeist encourages streetcar poetry;
differences are celebrated. Muslims welcome.

Queers and hippies, hipsters, all welcome.
Brown ones, pinkos, punks and Commies,

anarchists and lovelies, lonelies and uglies,
Democrats and Republies, all welcome.

C.S. Lewis at the wheel, elbow patches,
herringbone jacket;

learning to drive the right lane, a divorce
of grinding gears.

Ken Kesey and the Merry Pranksters tilt and jostle
to see. Every bench-seat becomes a balcony.

LSD. Lean on dashboard, lift a scuff toed parade boot
and read, read to the Holy Ghost of Rosa Parks

who sits defiant at the front. Not getting up
for anybody, sitting down, for everybody.

At the rear, those hollow sunken eyes,
he's dropped the Supertramp alias,

at peace now, accepting fate;
that's Chris MacCandless, emaciated,

93

still smiling. We weave through the hardscrabble
to the Haight. This is our stop.

Your president speaks in farts! I shout.
An ugly lizard, he's taking us all to Grey Town.

We are not at the foothills to Paradise, looking up,
we're staring into the abyss? Get on, hang on,

Bus No 1051,
the old green and cream,

part of this *mise en abyme*. This is where
I'll show you America.

On this San Francisco streetcar, dedicated to you
Harvey Milk, the Mayor of Castro Street.

Three steps down,
pirouette, doff my hat and bow.

ACKNOWLEDGEMENTS

My thanks to teachers in general, and a few who have had a profound influence on my life and writing: These are Professor Bob Spree, Coach Wayne Hager, Dr. Doug Mantz, and Mr. Jason MacPhail.

Blessings to Chris Needham and NON Publishing, Vancouver.

My hearty appreciation for the gift of Mark Sampson, for years of tireless encouragement, miles of edit work, and perseverance.

My gratitude to Nic Lupien, Kai Gosling, Rich Mears, and all the field team members and supporters of our work in Haiti. *Te moen se moen.*

My love to Corrine and Finley for teaching me about the good and for being the Big Bosses of my world.